Spend It or Save It?

by John Serrano

How Do People Earn Money?

Many people earn money by doing their jobs. The author who wrote this book earned money.

Look at the photos in this book. The people who took these photos also earned money.

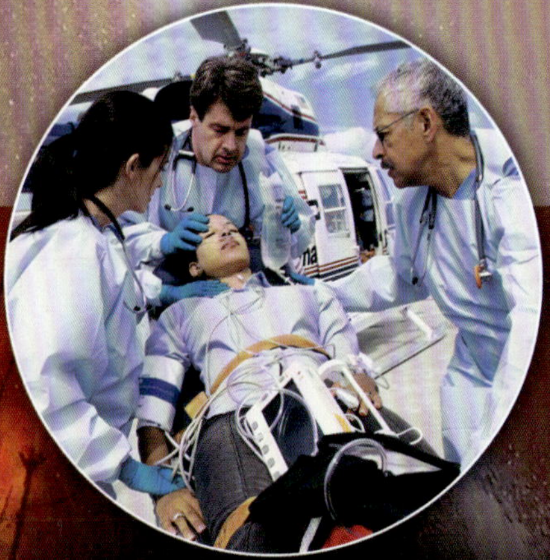

▲ People do many different jobs.

Some kids have jobs. This boy and girl rake leaves to help their neighbors. The neighbors give the kids money for helping.

These kids help their ▶ neighbors take care of their lawns.

This boy shovels snow to help his neighbors. The boy earns money for the work he does.

▲ This boy shovels snow so his neighbors don't slip and fall.

Where Do People Put Money?

People put money where they can keep the money safe. If you put your money in a safe place, you won't lose it.

A wallet is a safe place to keep your money when you will spend it soon. Your pocket is another safe place to put your money.

▲ This girl keeps money in her wallet.

A piggy bank is a safe place to put money. This girl saves some of her money in a piggy bank at home. She takes money out when she wants to buy something.

Some people save their money in a different kind of bank. This kind of bank holds money for many people.

◀ People go to this bank when they want to spend some of the money they have saved.

Why Do People Spend Money?

People spend money to buy things they need. People spend money on food and clothes.

▲ These people are buying food and clothes.

People spend money to get from place to place. A trip on the train costs money. A car and the gas in a car also cost money.

▲ People spend money on transportation.

Some people spend money on things they like to do. Going to see a movie costs money.

If you have a snack ▶ at the movies, you spend more money.

People spend money on a place to live. Buying or renting a home costs money. Using the lights and the water also cost money.

▲ You can spend less money by using less water and turning off the lights.

Why Do People Save Money?

People save money to buy things later. Homes and cars are some things people save money to buy.

Many people save money so they can go to school. These people want to learn more after high school.

Many people save money for college.

People make choices when they earn money. Will you save your money or will you spend some of it?